# HOW TO WRITE A BOOK AND PUBLISH ON AMAZON

## *MAKE MONEY WITH AMAZON KINDLE, CREATESPACE, AND AUDIOBOOKS*

ENTREPRENEUR PUBLISHING

# COPYRIGHT

# DISCLAIMER

# FREE GIFT

## Kindle 5 Star Books

## Free Kindle 5 Star Book Club Membership

Join Other Kindle 5 Star Members Who Are Getting Private Access To Weekly Free Kindle Book Promotions

## Get free Kindle books

Stay connected:

Join our Facebook group

Follow Kindle 5 Star on Twitter

Also, if you want to receive updates on Entrepreneur Publishing's new books, free promotions and Kindle countdown deals sign up to their New Release Mailing List.

For entrepreneurs: http://www.entrepreneurfinesse.com

# TABLE OF CONTENTS

**Introduction**

**Writing Your Content**

**Why Publish On Amazon?**

**Publishing on Kindle Direct Publishing (KDP)**

**Publishing On CreateSpace**

**Publishing on Audiobook Creation Exchange (ACX)**

**Conclusion**

# INTRODUCTION

Writing and publishing on Amazon can sound like a dream. It is actually an easy way to get your content out to the most readers as quickly as possible. However, you really must take the time to write quality content before you are ready to publish. Take a moment and consider why you want to publish your topic. Is it to make a name for yourself? Is it to educate the masses? Is it to share with the world an idea previously unwritten? These are all laudable reasons for wanting to publish. In fact, there are hundreds of reasons to want to publish and there's no reason why you can't self-publish through Amazon and get your work out to the world.

Create your content. Then publish on the Amazon platform of your choice using this handy guide. We will walk you through, page by page, how to publish on Kindle Direct Publishing and CreateSpace, and then you will learn how to create your own audiobooks through Audiobook Creation Exchange (ACX). With just this one guide, you have the keys to be able to publish on three high volume platforms and get your work out to the masses. These platforms are excellent ways to leverage both your writing and your time. Best of all, anyone can publish in the way they want and when they want. Exactly the way self-publishing should be.

# WRITING YOUR CONTENT

Before you can think about publishing, first you must create your content. This can be very easy or very hard, depending on the level of content you want to produce. If you have already produced some of your content, such as through blog posts or forum comments, it can be as simple as pulling the content together and putting it into a readable format. However, if you are starting off from scratch, this could take a while.

Creating content is simple. You choose a topic, do your research if there is any, write your content, and then publish it. However, the sticky part is often: do your research. This can take up quite a lot of time, especially if you want to insure your piece is exhaustively researched. Otherwise, if you are writing something such as fiction or nonfiction that you are well versed in, the path is quite a bit simpler. You pick out your topic and write your content.

For example, say you are writing a romance novel. The most you would need to know is how a romance typically goes and what the target word count is for your project. Then you can simply write away. However, if you're writing a historical romance novel, things can become a little stickier as you have to worry about being historically accurate to a certain degree. No plastic buttons on the dress, please.

The actual process of writing can be very systematic. In a lot of cases, it means to basically just sit down and write even if the terror of the blank page can be too much to handle. When starting out you may wish to sit down and first outline what you would like to talk about and take a few notes either from your head or from your research to help you get that first page started. This is a good way to start any book, first decide what you want to say and what category it falls in.

For example, this book works on publishing for the entrepreneurial minded. The reader wants to get their work out there in the eyes of the public. It has a slightly different bent from a book on publishing written solely for the fiction market. Once you decide on subject matter and category, a few notes are in order to bring forth the best ideas for you to cover in writing your content. These notes are your brainstorming session, so don't worry if they're not completely functional. You want to get your ideas down on paper so that they will be there when you're ready to get started.

Take the time to write out your notes. You can always edit them into shape later if you need to, but at first the trick is to just get them out there. You can do this by free writing. Free writing is when you start to write without an end in mind and simply allow your mind to go where it wishes to go. It can offer some great insights into what you really want to talk about. Also, if you don't mind taking a few days to get your thoughts together, you might try carrying around a notebook to record your thoughts about the project so that you can peruse it for gems later. You may even write portions of the work ahead of time while you're inspired. You could even take a tape recorder and dictate your notes onto digital format for your use later. All of these ways can help you to get your notes down so you will have something to work from once you start writing.

With those notes in hand, you are ready to start writing. Someone once said if you want to write a book, you should go someplace boring. You may just want to go somewhere that you aren't likely to be interrupted repeatedly. This could be your home office, the local coffee shop, the library, or any number of places. Just choose a place where you can hear yourself think and get words down on either paper or screen. Unless it is a very short book, you will probably be writing it in more than one session, so you want your sessions to be as focused as they can be. That means no randomly surfing the Internet looking for more research or to play PopCap games. Settle yourself down and really focus on your writing.

In order to get your writing done, use the Pomodoro technique, a specific way of managing time to allow you to get a lot done. It requires you to work for 25 minutes and take a five-minute break, before starting to work again for another 25 minutes. Once you have done four segments of 25 minutes, you can take a longer break of 15-30 minutes. This is a useful way to structure your writing time. The Pomodoro technique uses a simple kitchen timer to keep track of the time you spend working or resting. You could easily adapt your phone's timer app for that purpose. There are also a myriad of Internet apps, which can be used for the same purpose such as Focus Booster. This technique can be used on any length of time that you want, so don't feel as if you have to go with the traditional 25 minutes. Set it for 30 minutes, an hour, an hour and a half - it's all up to you.

If you can sit for longer, then by all means, sit for longer. Just make sure you quit writing before you've completely lost steam for the day. If you find yourself rereading the same passage you've written over and over, you are done, no more usable writing is going to come out of you. The next time you have time to write, refer to your notes and the last bit that you wrote previously to get an idea of where you were and what the next step is. This can save you a lot of writing in circles as you get yourself together.

After you've put together your content, you want to ensure it is in the best shape possible for publication. This may mean hiring an editor or making a pass at editing yourself to ensure you are putting out a quality product. There's nothing quite as galling as suddenly realizing you have a typo in a printed manuscript. One way to go about editing is to think of it as several passes over the book. In the first pass, you should consider all the major things you want to change content-wise, including the placement of chapters and the viability of ideas. In the second pass, you should be looking for whether or not the entire thing holds together the way that you want it to. On the third and final pass, consider grammar mistakes and typos. You may wish to add a fourth pass to double-check your research for all the research you chose to use. Make sure all quotes are right and attributed and that the numbers are correct. One popular tip for editing is to print out the manuscript in its entirety and make your corrections on the paper copy so that you aren't changing and then rechanging things in your primary document.

Once you've edited to the best of your ability, or someone else's, then you are ready to format your book for publication. The formatting is different depending on the platform you're using, so refer to the following sections for how to format for Kindle Direct, CreateSpace, and Audiobook Creation Exchange.

**Tip:** If you already know what format you are going to use, set up to use that format from the beginning of the writing process. This eliminates having to reset your work into the format later on and can save you a serious headache.

If you write from paper to computer, you are going to be tempted to change things around to make them sound better - this is fine. You can and should make changes to your manuscript to make it sound its best.

If you find yourself needing to do more research, do it at a time that is not your writing time. Keep research and writing separate as much as possible so that you're not wasting writing time doing research or distracted by writing while trying to research.

# WHY PUBLISH ON AMAZON?

With the proliferation of online publishing tools, choosing which one to publish on can be a daunting task. You want to ensure your book will get the greatest exposure. However, you also want ease of use, so that you're not fumbling around trying to make heads or tails of a confusing website. What you're looking for is exposure and ease of use.

*Amazon has both of those throughout its offerings in the publishing world.*

First, the level of exposure Amazon offers is exceedingly high. With millions of users worldwide, it is hard to cast a wider net than Amazon has for catching buyers. When people think of online shopping Amazon is more than likely the first place to look. While it can sometimes be hard to be seen with the vast collections of books that are published every day, with the right marketing, you can leverage Amazon's network into massive exposure for your book.

Secondly, let's talk about ease of use. Because there are so many people who want to publish through the Amazon platform, the corporate monolith has made it as simple as possible to publish through them. The directions are straightforward. Format your book in a readable congruent way. Everything is spelled out in their guides. YouTube is also a great resource to find more information in how to publish, format and market your books. And if you still somehow find it difficult, there is always the option of paying someone else to fix your problem. The process couldn't be simpler.

After considering these two important factors, it is easy to see why publishing on Amazon would be the right way to go for your business offering.

# Publishing on Kindle Direct Publishing (KDP)

Publishing with Kindle Direct Publishing is exactly what it sounds like; it is publishing for the Kindle, Amazon's ebook reader, a very popular electronic text reading device. While avoiding the headaches involved with formatting a book for CreateSpace, it is a quick way to get your book on Amazon and thus into the hands of readers. In fact, the turnaround publishing time on Kindle Direct is about 24-48 hours making it the fastest of the three options. You also have the option of changing or updating your book at any time. The changes will be automatically sent out to each of the files already published on Kindle devices. This means you can update with new content whenever you want. Combined with a royalty structure that is quite generous, giving as much as 70%, Kindle Direct Publishing seems like the way to go when you want to go fast, easy, and digital.

As with all three options, you must have a digital copy of your work that you wish to publish. While there are a number of formats available for you to use, it is recommended that you format your file as either a Word doc/docx or as HTML. One file type to stay away from is PDF. This is not to say that PDF cannot be used to convert into a Kindle book, just that it is more fraught with conversion issues than the others. You want to keep this quick and easy. Having to deal with a file that didn't convert correctly because of its file type isn't the way to keep it quick and easy. Other things you want to avoid because it will cause a problem in conversion are: bullet points, special characters, headers, and footers. None of these will convert, so don't use them in your finished product.

What about images? Both images and tables are available for use on the most recent version of the Kindle app, so you can add them to your book. Just keep in mind that people will be reading your book on a variety of devices. Make sure the table is truly necessary before you include it.

**BEFORE CONVERSION**

Things that you will need to add to your file before it is ready for conversion: Front matter, Back matter, and Table of Contents. These are essential to making your book look professional and well-done, so don't neglect to add them to your file. Front matter is important things like your title page, copyright page, dedication (optional), preface (optional), and prologue (which generally applies to fiction books). While you could certainly choose not to add all of these, the title page and the copyright page must be added. In some cases, you may wish to add a disclaimer page as well. It is not typically considered necessary front matter; however, if you want to ensure that others know your work is not to be tampered with – include it.

Your title page should, of course, contain the title of the book and the author or authors if others were involved in creating the work. Immediately following that is your copyright page. In the interest of time, I have included sample text for your copyright page.

- Copyright © 2015

This is a sample of what your copyright should read in order to protect your rights as the holder of the copyright under the law. Always make sure that the year reflected in the copyright is the year the book was published so the information is correct.

Once you've finished with the front matter, including deciding whether or not to add a disclaimer page, you are ready to work on the back matter. Back matter is things like glossaries, indexes, or notes, which are often found in the back of a text. This may not be necessary for you. If you don't have anything to put there, you don't have to make anything up. You can simply end on a blank page. However, in the interest of marketing, it is best to use the back matter as a place to offer connection points with your reader, or to preview another piece of work. On the last page of the book, include a short author's biography, your online handles so that others can get in touch with you, and, if possible, an excerpt from another piece you've publishing or have published. This is a good way to turn a customer into a valuable repeat customer.

Your table of contents is also the navigation page for your book. There are no page numbers, so it can be awfully hard to find a particular spot in a digital book. Your table of contents allows you to, at least somewhat, mitigate that problem. Now if you are using Word, it can create an active Table of Contents for you. That is one of its functions. However, if you're not using Word, you can still create one using the hyperlink and bookmark functions. For each chapter of your book, including the first page, the table of contents, and the last page, you will need to add bookmarks so the file can find them easily. Each section you will need in the Table of Contents should be labeled as a 'Header 1' in your word processor. You may have to try out a few things before you get it completely under your belt, but it shouldn't take long.

Here is a great video guide to learning how to format your ebook for Kindle: https://youtu.be/8sMzotvhGQg

With your front matter, back matter, and table of contents all taken care of you can look at the book as a whole and make decisions about whether or not you want to indent each of your paragraphs or what overall font you want to use. It is best to be consistent with the use of fonts to improve the reader experience. Your formatting should represent an enjoyable visual experience. Keep in mind as you go through your book that special characters will not convert and overly elaborate formatting is likely to get squashed into shape. You don't want to go through all this trouble only to have to do it again because one page didn't turn out right.

After formatting your document so that it is precisely what you want, it is imperative to also edit for proper grammar, punctuation and spelling. You should wait this long to do so because now you have already added everything you were going to add and can comb through the additional pieces as well and see the book as how a reader would view it.

Now you are ready to convert your file into the finished ebook.

### LOGGING IN AND THE BOOK DETAILS PAGE

In order to convert your file into your ebook, you first need to log into your Amazon account. It is okay if you don't have one, you just need to sign up for one at Amazon.com. Once you're logged in, you want to travel to the Kindle Direct Publishing page at http://kdp.amazon.com. There you will find a button that says 'Sign In'. It's on the right hand side and orange. Click on the button to get to your bookshelf. Since you haven't published anything before it will be empty, but that's not a problem.

Click on the 'Add New Title' button on the left hand side of the screen. This will bring you to a page, which asks for your book's details. All of the sections you can skip are labeled optional. Make sure you add yourself as a contributor to your book; otherwise, you won't be able to complete the page. You may wish to write your description out in a separate place so that you can reuse it during your promotional process. You also have to include categories under which your book can be found. Be as specific as you can as that will drop the number of books found under the same category allowing you more exposure. In the same vein, select your keywords carefully. You don't want them to be too general or you will be included in a very large pool of books.

Finally, there is your cover. You have two options: either have a cover made outside of Amazon or use their cover creator to create your cover at the time you make your book. Both options are good ones; however, if you want more control over how your book looks, you will want to have the cover created outside of Amazon so that you can upload the file along with your book document.

Some options for getting your book cover created are to hire your own graphic designer or use a website such as Fiverr. Some good places to find a quality designer for graphic design work are 99designs, elance and odesk.

## KINDLE DIRECT PUBLISHING SELECT

On the same page, at the top, is a discussion of Kindle Direct Publishing Select or KDP Select. This program will make your book exclusive to Kindle for a minimum of 3 months; however, it offers the enticing benefits of reaching more readers, earning more money, and maxing out your sales potential. It does this by giving you premium access to Amazon's markets in other parts of the world through Kindle Unlimited and Kindle Owners' Lending Library or KOLL. This gives you a better chance of reaching more readers. You earn more money through being eligible for KDP Select's Global Fund, which you will receive a portion of every time your book is selected and read more than ten percent or it is checked out through KOLL. It also allows you to get the 70% royalty on books sold in Mexico, India, Brazil and Japan. Finally, in order to maximize your sales potential, KDP Select offers the ability to run Countdown deals and Free deals for your book. This allows you to change the price of your book for limited amounts of time, thus appealing to more readers. You have to decide whether or not you would like to enroll your book in KDP Select. As long as you don't publish your book elsewhere, including your website or your blog, you are able to enroll the book later in KDP Select. Once you've entered all the information required on the Book Details page, you can preview how your book will look. Take some time and look at the preview before you move on to the Rights and Pricing page.

### RIGHTS AND PRICING

Now that you've made it to the Rights and Pricing page, the first thing the website wants you to do is select the territories for which you hold the rights to publish this book. In most cases, you won't need to do anything here, unless the book is under copyright in another country already. Next it offers you the option of KDP Pricing Support. This feature shows you how other books of the same type did and at what price point they were set. This is useful if you don't know what you want to sell your book for.

After that, you come to the options for royalties. There are two: 35% and 70%. They are different because the 70% option has delivery costs associated with it. It also is not available on ebooks that are either below $2.99 or above $9.99. At the 35% rate, there are no delivery costs. Prices between $0.99 and $200.00 are available at the 35% royalty rate. Choose whichever royalty rate is right for you and go down the screen to where it offers you the chance to put in a list price. Once you input the list price it will tell you not only what the list price will be in all the listed territories, but it will also tell you the delivery cost associated with your book for each territory. If the delivery cost is high, you may wish to go with the 35% royalty option. After you've chosen your royalty rate and list price, you are essentially finished. There are two other programs at the bottom of the page, which Amazon offers which you may wish to enroll your book in. One is Kindle MatchBook and the other is Kindle Book Lending.

Kindle Matchbook only applies if you also have a print version of your book such as through CreateSpace. It allows those users who have purchased your print book to also purchase your Kindle edition at a reduced cost. This can be useful for getting repeat business. Also, Kindle Book Lending allows your book to be lent out for a maximum of 14 days. This allows you to be further previewed and will help to increase sales.

You have now reached the bottom of the page. You have two options: Save and Publish or Save as Draft. If you're ready for your book to go live and you've made all the changes to it that you need to, your cover is in place, and you are absolutely sure, click Save and Publish. Keep in mind, you can always come back and update the book edition later if need be. Just don't make that an excuse to put forth an unfinished product just to have one on the market. Save as Draft allows you to save everything you have done for publication at a later date. This could be useful if you're waiting on something to be completed such as the cover.

If you clicked Save and Publish, now all you have to do is wait for the email confirmation from Amazon that your book has gone live in order to get the URL from which your book will be sold. The email typically takes 12-24 hours to arrive. Congratulations you have successfully published a book on Kindle!

# PUBLISHING ON CREATESPACE

Of the three platforms, CreateSpace is the only one you have to sign into a separate website from Amazon for. CreateSpace is a platform for making a print copy of your book. This can be useful if you would like to have copies for public appearances. In order to use CreateSpace, you must create a profile at their website (http://www.CreateSpace.com). When you first log in, you will see your bookshelf, currently without any titles. Click on the 'Add a Title' button in order to start creating your title.

There are two setup process options – guided and expert. They both need the same information except expert is more streamlined yet however it provides lackluster help for what each section does. Expert is recommended after you have published a couple of books through CreateSpace.

The first page you will come to is the Title Information page. This is where you enter the basic information on your title, including the title itself, the author information, edition number, whether or not your book is part of a series, language, and publication date. If you leave publication date blank, it will auto populate with the date when your book is ready for print. At the bottom of the page, 'Save and Continue'.

## ISBN

The next page is the ISBN page. If you have already purchased an ISBN this is where you would put it in. If you haven't, you have a couple of choices. You can have CreateSpace assign you one for your book, you can purchase a custom one, or you can buy a custom universal. You don't have to make this decision immediately, but it must be done before you publish your book. If you choose the CreateSpace ISBN then your ISBN is only good through CreateSpace and CreateSpace is shown as your imprint of record. It does not affect your distribution because you can still use all of the available distribution channels.

If you want to go a little fancier, for $10 you can purchase a custom ISBN that will allow you to choose your imprint of record. The custom ISBN is still only good through CreateSpace. You could also purchase a Custom Universal

ISBN which would be good on any publisher (including CreateSpace) and allows you to choose your imprint of record. A good option depending on what it is you are trying to do. If you are unfazed about having CreateSpace appear as your imprint of record, then go ahead and take the cheapest route. However, if you are planning on publishing multiple books, it may be worth it to purchase at a higher rate in order to have the imprint of record be the same on all your books.

### INTERIOR

If you choose not to make a decision about ISBN at this time, you can navigate away from that page by using the left hand toolbar to move on to interior. Here is where you would choose your interior details and upload your file. Your interior details depend on whether or not you have color graphics in your book. If you have color graphics, you will choose color. If not, then choose black and white. Black and white can choose either white or cream colored paper. Should you be worried about what the paper actually looks like you can order a sample from CreateSpace so that you can see what the pages will look like. This is also where you chose your trim size. Trim size is the size your book will be once all the manufacturing changes have been made. It's the size the book will be in your hands. You can choose from a number of industry standard sizes to allow you to create a book that is the right size for what you want. Once you've chosen your trim size, it is in your best interest to download the Word Template for that trim size because it will make getting your file in shape a lot easier. Once you have the template, you can simply copy and paste your book into the template and upload that as your interior.

In case you would rather not go through creating your interior yourself, CreateSpace offers Professional design services for this section starting at $199. You can turn your manuscript over to a professional and they will make sure your manuscript has a perfectly formatted interior.

For writers who want to save time and money I would recommend converting your book from word into PDF using a service such as http://smallpdf.com/

Going on your own though, you would upload your document, with the appropriate margins for your trim size into the website. It will take some time to go through the document looking for obvious places where there is a problem such as text that falls outside of the visible margins or text that falls into the gutter. The gutter is the section of your book along the spine which will be hidden from view once the book is put together. The Interior Reviewer, a tool of the website, will review your book and show you where the problems are. If the problems are such that you would need to revamp your project, you can make changes to the Word document and re-upload it to start the review process all over again. However, if the problems are minor, or won't cause any damage to the completed manuscript's printing, then you can ignore the problems and move forward.

## COVER

The next step is to put together the cover. You have three options when it comes to covers: use your own, create one using Cover Creator, or use the design services that start at $399. Having an artist create a cover for you gives you the most creative freedom where your cover is concerned. Keep in mind that covers for CreateSpace and covers for Kindle look very different. One is a single plate cover for an ebook, the other is a full cover for a print book. They can look much the same, but the amount of space to cover is quite different. Keep that in mind when looking for a cover artist. If you want to use the Cover Creator, it loads directly from the cover page and gives you a number of options to choose from. Take your time and build the best cover you can using the options available if you chose to go this route. If you would rather a professional did the work for you, you can use the Design Services available from this page as well. Keep in mind this will lengthen the amount of time that it takes to get your book out in print because there will be putting together the cover, then verifying, and finally accepting. Budget the time accordingly. Again, finding a graphic designer for this step is highly recommended.

Once you have finished your cover, you are now ready to send your book off to be reviewed by the CreateSpace staff. After sending your book off for review in about 12 hours you'll receive an email regarding the next steps toward the completion of your manuscript.

The last step is to proof your book. Look through the pages of your book carefully as the projected book reflects how the pages will look in print. Once you approve the book, it will go live within the Amazon store in 3-5 days.

## Distribution

While you're waiting on that email, you can take a look at the Distribution channels available to you. You are automatically enrolled in the CreateSpace eStore, Amazon.com, and Amazon Europe. You could also, following the review process, be eligible for CreateSpace Direct, Bookstores and Online retailers, and Libraries & Academic Institutions. However, these are expanded distribution channels and not absolutely necessary so don't worry about them too much. I would still recommend choosing every distribution channel, as you want the most exposure for your book. Click 'Save' at the bottom of the page. After finishing Distribution, you can move on to the Pricing.

## Pricing

In Pricing, the first thing you will notice is that they give you a minimum list price for your book. This is so that you will actually make royalties on your title. Create On Demand means that you will pay for each book as it is printed. You have to use this price at minimum in order to be able to publish your book. It is non-negotiable. Once you've put in the amount you would like to sell for, then the system will automatically populate the information for royalties based on your distribution channels. All you have to do at this point is 'Save'.

## Description

Despite the fact that the next thing on the list is Cover Finish, you've already selected that on another page, so you can move on to Description. You need to make sure you have a compelling description of your book to grab your reader's attention. This will help to move your book off the shelves. Take some time and truly make sure you have as good a description as you can manage. Following that is the BISAC category, that stands for Book Industry Standards and Communication. It is asking what category your book belongs in, choose the most detailed category you can that describes your book. On this page, you can also add an Author Biography. This is where you can put any information on your qualifications or awards for the public to see. It only shows up on certain distribution channels, however.

## PUBLISH TO KINDLE

Finally, after going through all of those steps, you reach the last one, which you may have already completed. CreateSpace allows you to publish on Kindle Direct Publishing using the same files you have already put together for them. All you have to do is finish the review process and they will send your work from one platform to the other. This can save you a lot of time, if you're going to be putting together both a print and Kindle book. You only have to truly complete the process once.

After your book has been reviewed and verified by those at CreateSpace, it will be time for you to take a look at it and make sure that it is exactly what you wanted. To do this, you will receive a proof copy of your book from CreateSpace and look it over to insure you intended for the spacing to look the way it does, to perhaps catch any last minute errors. If you're not happy, fix your upload file and re-upload it, which will start the process over again. If you are happy with it, you simply notify CreateSpace through your account and they will put your book up for sale within 1 to 2 business days.

# PUBLISHING ON AUDIOBOOK CREATION EXCHANGE (ACX)

Audiobook Creation Exchange is another Amazon platform specifically for the creation of audiobooks. Rights holders and producers are able to collaborate and publish audiobooks through this platform. Audiobooks are by far the longest route to creating a finished project and also the one that is the most out of your hands. However, that does not mean it's a bad way to go, only that you have to be prepared to have a little less hands on experience with this platform unless you choose to produce your audiobook yourself.

### CREATING YOUR AUDIOBOOK IF YOU'RE GOING TO USE A NARRATOR/PRODUCER

It is best that you already have a print or Kindle version of your book already out there before you attempt to create an audiobook because that makes it easier for ACX to find you. Once you have found your book through the ACX search function, you click on "This is my book". Depending on what you choose, whether to produce your book yourself or to find a narrator and producer for your book, you will be prompted to sign in with your Amazon account. You should already have an Amazon account if you created a Kindle book. Otherwise, you may need to set one up now. It doesn't take long. After you've logged in, ACX will ask for information on you as the Rights Holder of the book. When it comes to the dropdown menu, you are an author.

On the next page, you will be prompted to enter information regarding the book. Some of it will be auto-populated by the system because you have entered this information elsewhere. You can choose to enter the Copyright information at this time or wait until later. It will have to be done before the manuscript is sent to the producer however. After that, you're asked to provide more salient information about your book, such as if it is fiction or nonfiction and what category it falls into. Following that, you will be asked for your ideal narrator's voice, if you are choosing to have someone else narrate your book. Then you will need to also upload an audition script so that you can receive auditions based on the script you provide. You can only choose a portion of your manuscript to use, so choose a part you want to ensure is read well so that you can use that as your benchmark for how well the narrators do. Click 'Save and Continue' to move on.

At the top of the next page, it asks for the overall word count of your project so that it can estimate the amount of finished time the audiobook will have. This can also help determine your price so be accurate. You should, since you haven't entered into a contract with anyone, still have World distribution rights for your audiobook. Now we come down to something very important, payment. You can either choose to share the royalties or to pay upfront for the production of your audiobook. Both of these have their pluses and minuses. If you pay for it upfront, there is more upfront cost to you but all royalties thereafter will go directly to you. ACX has a 40% royalty rate for exclusive rights and a 25% rate for non-exclusive rights, which you will find out a little further down. Choosing to share royalties means less upfront cost, but also less royalties down the line. Choose whichever seems the best at the time and remember you will get to make this decision each time you work on an audiobook, so it is truly a one-off decision. Once you have chosen your payment structure, you have to choose exclusive or non-exclusive rights. This determines where your book will be distributed. If you want to stick with the three platforms that ACX offers, Audible, Amazon, and iTunes, then choose the exclusive rights option which comes with the 40% royalty package. If you think you want to distribute your audiobook through other channels, then you would choose non-exclusive and the 25% royalty rate.

Once you've again clicked 'Save and Continue' you will be brought to a summary page which will list the information you already entered and ask if you want to post to ACX so that narrators can audition for your book. If you are certain you are ready, then click 'Post to ACX'. If you want to think about it a little more or perhaps make changes later, 'Save and Continue Later'. If you don't like what you see and what to make changes now 'Edit Profile'.

Once you have posted the work to ACX, the next thing you do is wait. It will take time for the auditions to come in for your work. Once the auditions are in, you can listen to them and choose your favorite. Following that, you will enter into an agreement with your new narrator to produce the project. They will narrate the book and you will get a chance to listen and ask for corrections before your book goes live. Then it just comes down to promoting it.

### Choosing to be Your Own Narrator

If you would prefer to have more control over this process, instead of using the audition system and picking out a narrator and producer, you have the option of narrating your book yourself and uploading the audio. This requires more work upfront, but once you've done it once, you know how to do it again for your next audiobook. This also allows you to jump the several week process of choosing a narrator and producer for your book.

There are several good resources for setting up your own home studio, which will help you get started. Overall, one would need to learn how to perform simple recording and audio production/mastering. Once you are ready to upload your project, you simply log into ACX using your Amazon account, choose 'Add your Title', fill in the metadata (things such as author, copyright dates, etc.), and book description, and 'Continue'. You will be prompted to upload your audio files including your opening and closing credits, chapters, and sample audio file, which will be used to preview your book for new listeners. Once you've uploaded your audio files, click 'I'm Done' in the upper right hand corner. You can also add cover art from this screen. I would suggest using the same or similar cover art from the book itself.

While it is a time consuming process, you can certainly prepare and upload your own audiobook in your spare time to take advantage of the audiobook market. In fact, with this process one can monetize their microphone and vocal chords through narrating other rights holders audiobooks.

# CONCLUSION

That was a lot of information to absorb, but we just covered three of the major Amazon publishing platforms. You should now be ready to publish tackle any problem that Kindle Direct Publishing, CreateSpace or ACX throw your way. I hope this book was able to help you feel more comfortable with the idea of publishing your own work through Amazon so that you can reach the audience eagerly awaiting your book.

To hear about Entrepreneur Publishing's new books first (and to be notified when there are free promotions), sign up to their New Release Mailing List.

Finally, if you enjoyed this book, please take the time to share your thoughts and post a review on Amazon. It'd be greatly appreciated!

THANK YOU AND GOOD LUCK!

# PREVIEW OF 'HOW AUDIOBOOKS MAKE YOU SMARTER' FROM ENTREPRENEUR PUBLISHING

## Hearing Is The Primary Resource For Retention

*In this chapter, you will learn:*

- Key parts of the ear, now they work together, and

- Understanding the auditory nervous system.

### AUDITORY FUNCTION IS CONSTANT

As you may know, the one sense we nearly all would list as the one we would hate to lose is vision. We are so dependent on sight that we quite often fail to recall that unlike sight, the primary sense upon which we depend on the most is our hearing.

Hearing impacts every one of us, every day, in a myriad of ways. Most often, we only concentrate on the specifics we might listen for - danger, our loved ones, or beautiful sounds such as those of nature or music.    But what we don't always realize are those functions that interact with the outside world.

Learning, therefore, will always have a function in the learning process. The more we can incorporate hearing in the process, the more natural that learning process becomes, because we are tying that which we do as a matter of living into that which can improve out individual lives. Thus, we create a positive and recursive learning spiral, improving for the purpose of increasing the desire to improve.

### HEARING AS A FUNCTION OF BALANCE

While we usually don't consider it, the speed of the wind, the stability of the soil, even the proximity of perils can be reacted to if we are hearing properly. Not only the audible sounds themselves, but also the movement and pressure of the air around us provide the feedback correlation necessary between the gyroscopic nature of the inner ear, and our cognition of our surroundings    While it wouldn't seem to make a direct relationship, the ability for us to learn is dependent on that balance feature, because without the ability to coordinate what we are hearing with our other sensory inputs, we literally couldn't walk and chew bubble gum at the same time.

To understand why the auditory process in general, and audiobooks in particular can improve our learning processes, and improve our intellect, we first have to have an understanding of how we, as human beings, store memories. While science and medicine have yet to unlock these mysteries, a great deal can be understood if we think about our own learning process.

## OPTICAL

When we look at something, we have the capacity to hold that vision, and continually receive verification of it, of the data it represents again and again. In the case of learning, we can even review it more than a singular experience.   The need for speed in this process is clear; there is a lot to see, and our brains need to process quickly. Thus, memories supplant what we actually see with symbols and the interconnection between them. Retention of these long-term symbols and the interrelationship between them is called **iconic memory.** The conversion process from visual to iconic memory is rapid, and that is why what we see and what we retain are usually very small percentages of our learning; it is sheer repetition and continuous learning that embeds the information for later recall.

## AUDITORY

Hearing, on the other hand, is a very different kind of mental input. Unlike sight, wherein one can continue to take in information, and even visually review such input, sounds generally are 'hearable' a single time. In the mind, therefore, a sound has to be maintained in memory, effectively, as an echo of the sound itself.   Thus, when we recall a sound, a noise, or even words, our brains fundamentally recall the specific sound as a 're-play' of it. That is to say, the actual sound response is held, not as the cognizant representation (as in optic memories) but as what is now known as **'echoic memory'.** The term was coined in 1967, by Uric Neisser, who was doing research on how audial memory is retained. In essence, the brain captures a sound (almost literally as we describe audibly memorable information) fundamentally as a sound byte, that it holds and replays for access, until the brain can interconnect it with experiences and the iconic memory. This process, mentally, is longer; we only get the singular input, but the brain retains the specifics longer. (Neisser, U. (1967). Cognitive psychology. Englewood Cliffs: Prentice-Hall. ISBN 978-0131396678)

It is precisely because this memory function operates differently, that the auditory and visual learning methods should be both employed to enhance learning overall. Utilizing an auditory learning process can increase knowledge retention, as the information is not only connected to your mental associations through Optic processes, but also through a secondary sensory means. This gives your mind an alternate, and hopefully amplified means to keep and maintain information.

In particular, as the segmentation of what we see is so fast, so broad, and so much more processed than that of what we hear, the benefit of the audiobook over the written book is defined by the amount of retention of the original data. It is true that one can review, and review the material if it is written, but the review functions to reinforce the secondary phase, the iconic memory. When we listen to a source, we capture bigger 'chunks' of the information, and retain it in that original form, without filter or interpretation. Access, therefore is faster, because the data does not have to be re-correlated, reconnected for the thought, the memory to make sense.

### COGNITION AND MEMORY
In this section, we are going to get down to the brass tacks about memory, and how iconic memory, echo memory, intentional mnemonics and sound theory call play into creating a 'perfect storm' of learning opportunity.

### SIGNAL TO NOISE RATIO (WHAT YOU HEAR VS. HOW WELL YOU LISTEN)
There is a very well known difference between hearing someone, and listening to them. In like fashion there is a distinct difference between noise (stuff you hear) and signal (stuff you are trying to listen to). When the actual ratio between these gets too off balance, then learning ceases. So it is best to determine what that ratio is for you, and then work to maintain the balance in order to maximize your learning output.

### WORKING MEMORY VS. LONG-TERM MEMORY VS. DATA RETRIEVAL
Functionally, learning consists of three types of memory. Long-term memory is a function of life experiences and situations, wherein we can gather that information when necessary, even if it occurred long ago. Data Retrieval is the memory process we use often, to pull out significant data from our mental records, and fundamentally ensure we can access everything smoothly. Working memory is that part of the brain's function where we discern and make conclusions, and draw up plans and otherwise work with the data from the other two sources. Hearing feeds directly into long-term memory, so it is a matter of training the Data Retrieval processes to rapidly deploy them, and for the Working memory to be able to manipulate them.

### MEMORY AND ENCRYPTION THROUGH SOUND VS. OPTICS
A recent film had a scene where a data file was encrypted with images and sounds, to make the retrieval a challenge to do without the precise images and specific sound sequence.

In reality, that is how memory works. One finds a piece of information useful, and decides to commit it to memory. We associate that piece of information with the current details, like sounds, sights, feelings, and we log it away with all those details, so we can access it later.

Then, as we require it, we use our minds to determine where it is in memory, connect the dots, as it were, and then pull it back for working memory use.

Click here to check out the rest of How Audiobooks Make You Smarter on Amazon.

Or go to: http://amzn.to/1BXwtqm

# More Books for Entrepreneurs

Click here to check out the rest of Entrepreneur Publishing's books on Amazon.

Below you'll find some of my other popular books that are popular on Amazon and Kindle as well. Simply click on the links below to check them out. Alternatively, you can visit my author page on Amazon to see other work done by me.

How Audiobooks Make You Smarter: 7 Little Known Ways Audio Books Can Boost Memory Capacity And Increase Intelligence

How To Write A Book And Publish On Amazon: Make Money With Amazon Kindle, CreateSpace And Audiobooks

If the links do not work, for whatever reason, you can simply search for these titles on the Amazon website to find them.